HM QUEEN ELIZABETH II

DIAMOND JUBILEE

A Royal Baby is Born

When Elizabeth was born into the Royal Family, she was never expected to one day be Queen.

Elizabeth was third in line to the throne behind her uncle, Edward, Prince of Wales, and her father.

Elizabeth was born at 2.40am on 21 April 1926 in London, the first child of the Duke and Duchess of York. She was given the name Elizabeth Alexandra Mary.

Princess Elizabeth

Elizabeth as a child

Her first name was after her mother, the second after her father's grandmother, Queen Alexandra, and the third after her father's mother, Queen Mary.

When Elizabeth was four, her sister, Margaret Rose, was born. The family were very close and spent many happy times together, often at Royal Lodge, their new home in Windsor Great Park.

Elizabeth and her sister, Margaret

The family in the grounds at Windsor Castle, 1936

A NEW ROLE FOR THE FAMILY

Elizabeth playing as a child

Princess Elizabeth or 'Lilibet', as she called herself, enjoyed a carefree childhood until she was ten. Then, her life was turned upside down. In January 1936, her grandfather King George V died and was succeeded by her uncle, King Edward VIII. He had reigned less than a year when he gave up the throne in order to marry an American divorcee. In 1936 it was impossible for the king to marry a divorced woman, and Edward was determined to be with Wallis Simpson. The crown passed to Elizabeth's father, who was crowned King George VI just before Christmas in 1936.

Elizabeth was now heir to the throne

With their father as King, the princesses had to get used to life in the spotlight. For the young Elizabeth, the unexpected change in royal succession would have enormous consequences. It meant that one day she would be Queen.

The coronation of King George VI

A War And
A Royal Wedding

Three years later, World War II broke out in 1939. The young princess was keen to help and, in early 1945, aged nineteen, she joined the Auxiliary Territorial Service (ATS). This was the women's branch of the Army. Elizabeth worked as a volunteer and by the end of the war in 1945, she was a Junior Commander and a qualified driver!

The royal bride and groom

Elizabeth first met her future husband, Prince Philip of Greece, when she was a bridesmaid at a royal wedding in 1934. During the war, Prince Philip, now an officer in the Royal Navy, and the princess kept in touch by letter. They later married at Westminster Abbey in November 1947. It was a simple occasion, as the country was still recovering from wartime restrictions. Coming after such a time of sadness, the excitement of a royal wedding was welcomed by people all around the world.

A Crowning Moment

On 6 February 1952, when Princess Elizabeth and Philip were mid-way through an African tour, they were told the sad news of her father's death. The tour was abandoned, and Elizabeth, aged just 25, flew back to England as Queen.

The coronation of Queen Elizabeth II took place at Westminster Abbey on 2 June 1953. It was a spectacular event, and Elizabeth took her vows with great dignity. Crowds lined the streets to catch a glimpse of their new Queen. The ceremony was broadcast on the radio and the event was also televised and watched by many people. Television was new in homes, so this was the first opportunity people had had to share in an event as it happened.

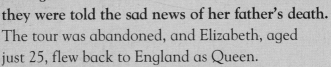

The coronation was reported around the world

Hundreds of people stood along the procession route

Of Elizabeth's children, only Prince Charles and Princess Anne had been born when she was crowned. After the ceremony, they joined the Queen on the balcony of Buckingham Palace, just as she and her sister had joined their parents after their father's coronation.

A New Royal Family

Prince Charles as a baby

Before Elizabeth became Queen, her first child, Prince Charles, was born at Buckingham Palace in 1948. Shops closed and people celebrated up and down the country. Then, in 1950, he was followed by a sister, Princess Anne. A second son, Prince Andrew, was born in 1960 and her fourth child, Prince Edward, was born in 1964.

Prince Charles and his sister, Princess Anne

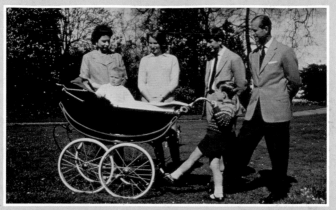

Prince Edward was the Queen's fourth child

When it was time to educate their children, Princess Elizabeth and Prince Philip broke with tradition by being the first members of the Royal Family to send their children to school. Elizabeth, by contrast, had been educated at home by governesses, and perhaps realized that the rough and tumble of the playground was a better introduction to the world for her children.

Prince Charles at prep school with friends, 1957

A Royal Life

As Head of State, the Queen had many new duties to perform. There were documents to read and sign, important ceremonies to attend and regular meetings with the Prime Minister.

The Queen reading documents at her desk in Buckingham Palace

The Queen delivers her first Christmas speech from Sandringham House, 1952

The Queen talking to a young well-wisher

Her Royal Highness, often with Prince Philip at her side, has visited more than 120 different countries around the world. She always seems perfectly comfortable whether addressing a crowd of thousands, or crouching to listen to the whispered words of a small child.

The Queen still undertakes about 430 engagements every year (more than one a day!) and travels the world on official state visits. As the years pass, she shows little sign of slowing down on her official duties, despite being in her eighties.

The Queen travels around the world meeting key dignitaries from many countries

The Queen Around the World

Her Majesty the Queen is not just Head of State in the United Kingdom. She is also Sovereign of 15 Commonwealth countries; Australia, New Zealand, Canada, Jamaica, Antigua and Barbuda, the Bahamas, Barbados, Grenada, Belize, St. Christopher and Nevis, St. Lucia, the Solomon Islands, Tuvalu, St. Vincent and the Grenadines and Papua New Guinea, as well as Head of the Commonwealth itself.

The Queen helps to connect all of these diverse nations and promote friendship and negotiation. It cannot always be easy, and there is a great deal of protocol to remember, but the Queen instinctively knows both how to greet a child in Australia and chat to the King of Tonga.

Queen Elizabeth receives King George Tupou V of Tonga at Buckingham Palace

In the United Kingdom, the Queen takes a caring interest in the state papers submitted to her each day and meets with the British Prime Minister every week. Although

The Queen and Winston Churchill, 1955

it is important that the Queen expresses no political views in public, this meeting is an opportunity for Her Majesty to express her thoughts on the current political situation and ask questions on particular topics.

The Queen and Prime Minister David Cameron, 2011

IMPORTANT EVENTS

The Queen's incredible 60 years of almost non-stop official visits and state occasions have been punctuated by some key moments. With her family, she has celebrated many happy events, but, like most people, has also suffered her fair share of sadness and tragedy.

Wonderful highlights for the Queen have been the marking of her Jubilees. The flags flew in 1977 to celebrate her Silver Jubilee, marking 25 years on the throne, then her Golden Jubilee, marking the 50th year of her reign, took place in 2002. Both happy occasions were marked by special events and large-scale tours.

The Queen on the balcony of Buckingham Palace during her Silver Jubilee celebrations

The Queen enjoyed a close relationship with her mother and sister

During 2002, the Queen and the Duke of Edinburgh visited 70 cities and towns in the UK over the summer months! However glorious the celebrations were, this was also a very sad time for Her Majesty, as both her sister and mother died within just seven weeks of each other at the start of the year. It must have saddened the Queen that neither her beloved mother or sister were there to share the celebrations of such an important year.

The Queen's Gold State Coach makes its way down the Mall during Her Majesty's Golden Jubilee celebrations

FAMILY OCCASIONS

In April 2011, the Queen and the rest of the world rejoiced in the marriage of Prince William to Catherine Middleton. It is clear that the Queen enjoyed the day tremendously. Her Majesty was involved in many aspects of the wedding preparations and details, and even advised her

The Duke and Duchess of Cambridge

grandson on the guest list, putting protocol aside, and telling him to start with his friends!

The Queen and the rest of the bridal party at the wedding of Prince William and Catherine Middleton

A second royal wedding in the summer of 2011 made the year even more remarkable. On a warm summer's day in July, the Queen's eldest granddaughter, Zara Phillips, married England rugby star Mike Tindall at a small ceremony in Edinburgh, Scotland.

The wedding was attended by members of the Royal Family, including the Queen, the newly-wed Duke and Duchess of Cambridge, and Prince Henry, known as Harry. The Queen enjoys spending time with her family and it must have been wonderful to be able to share two extremely happy events with so many family members.

Zara Phillips and Mike Tindall on their wedding day

Home and Creature Comforts

Buckingham Palace – the official royal residence

Over the centuries, Britain's kings and queens have built or bought palaces to serve as family homes. Buckingham Palace has been the official residence of Britain's sovereigns since 1837 and is still the administrative headquarters of the Queen and her immediate family.

Windsor Castle is the largest occupied castle in the world, and has been both a royal home and fortress for over 900 years.

The Queen often spends weekends at Windsor Castle and is always in residence over Easter and in June each year

When Her Majesty takes a private summer holiday, it is often to Balmoral Castle in Scotland. Similarly, Sandringham House in Norfolk is a

Sandringham House – private home to four generations of Sovereigns since 1862

favourite place and the Queen always spends Christmas here with members of her family.

The Queen and her beloved dogs

When on holiday or relaxing at home, the Queen is often seen with several dogs around her feet. She has always had a great love of animals. She enjoys riding horses, and owns and breeds thoroughbred racehorses. The Queen has also owned more than thirty corgis, and several dorgis (a cross between a corgi and a dachsund). Her first pet was a corgi called Susan, a present on her 18th birthday.

A Glittering Jubilee

Queen Victoria's Diamond Jubilee

The Diamond Jubilee in 2012 celebrates 60 years of the Queen's reign. It is only the second time Britain has celebrated such an event, the first being Queen Victoria's Diamond Jubilee in 1897.

Much like our present Queen will do, Victoria travelled to a thanksgiving service in an open carriage before returning to Buckingham Palace through the streets of London. In 2012, celebrations are planned across the country. The Queen will visit parts of the UK, while other members of the Royal Family will travel to 15 countries where she is Head of State, as well as other Commonwealth countries around the world.

The official £5 coin to mark Queen Elizabeth's Diamond Jubilee

The official emblem for the Jubilee celebrations

A competition held amongst school children to design the official emblem for the Jubilee was won by Katherine Dewar, aged 10, and will be seen all over the country in the lead up to the celebrations.

On Reflection

The Queen has reigned through 60 years of enormous social change and development, and has helped shape today's modern Royal Family. The monarchy now has its own website and you can even follow Her Majesty on Twitter! In addition, Buckingham Palace has been opened to the public and even the rules on curtseying have been relaxed.

A portrait of young Elizabeth

From a young age, the Queen knew that her destiny would be to guide her subjects with calm dignity through good times and bad, and it is a job she has undertaken faultlessly, elegantly and with a warm smile. May she continue to do so for years to come.

**Congratulations,
Your Majesty, on 60 glorious years.**